to

....

from

....

date

A Father's Prayer
©2014 by Jack Countryman

Published in Nashville, Tennessee, by Thomas Nelson.

Thomas Nelson titles may be purchased in bulk for educational, business, fund-raising, or sales promotional use. For information, please e-mail SpecialMarkets@ThomasNelson.com.

Scripture quotations are taken from the NEW KING JAMES VERSION®. © 1982 by Thomas Nelson. Used by permission. All rights reserved.

ISBN 978-0-7180-1657-9

Printed in the United States of America

14 15 16 17 18 POL 5 4 3 2 1

www.thomasnelson.com

A Father's Prayer

by
Jack Countryman

COUNTRYMAN®

A Division of Thomas Nelson Publishers

THOMAS NELSON®
Since 1798

NASHVILLE   DALLAS   MEXICO CITY   RIO DE JANEIRO

CONTENTS

A Father's Prayer

*Be anxious for nothing, but in everything by prayer
and supplication, with thanksgiving, let your requests
be made known to God; and the peace of God, which
surpasses all understanding, will guard your hearts
and minds through Christ Jesus.*

PHILIPPIANS 4:6–7

*F*ather, You are more precious to me than life. Thank You for the gift of salvation, which You so generously have given. Forgive me when I have failed to be the father You wish me to be. Pour out Your Spirit upon me so that I might boldly come to the throne of grace and find mercy and power in Your presence. You have blessed me with children and a family; guide me in my words and actions toward them. Shower me with the peace that passes all understanding. Guard my heart and mind so that each day I will be the father You desire me to be. *Amen.*

Listen *to the* Holy Spirit

*"If you ask anything in My name, I will do it.
If you love Me, keep My commandments. And
I will pray the Father, and He will give you
another Helper, that He may abide with you
forever—the Spirit of truth, whom the world
cannot receive, because it neither sees Him
nor knows Him; but you know Him, for He
dwells with you and will be in you."*

JOHN 14:14–17

You have given me a Helper, someone who will be with me in every circumstance of life. Heavenly Father, thank You for this gift that You have given to all who accept Jesus as their personal Savior. Help me learn to listen to Your Spirit and seek You with all my heart. You have promised to be my Comforter, to strengthen and guide me in every situation. I will keep Your commandments and look forward to meditating on Your Word as I walk through life. *Amen.*

A Father's Eternal Hope

*Blessed be the God and Father of our Lord Jesus
Christ, who according to His abundant mercy
has begotten us again to a living hope through the
resurrection of Jesus Christ from the dead, to an
inheritance incorruptible and undefiled and that
does not fade away, reserved in heaven for you,
who are kept by the power of God through faith
for salvation ready to be revealed in the last time.*

1 Peter 1:3–5

*L*ord, You are my hope. I know there
are challenges I will face, and my
faith may be tested. But I know You will be
with me, and nothing and no one can take
away Your presence. Even when times are
difficult and things seem hopeless, Your love
is everlasting. Even when I walk through the
darkest shadow, You will be with me. *Amen.*

I Need Your Wisdom

*Get wisdom! Get understanding! Do not forget,
nor turn away from the words of my mouth.
Do not forsake her, and she will preserve you;
love her, and she will keep you. Wisdom is the
principal thing; therefore get wisdom. And in all
your getting, get understanding.*

PROVERBS 4:5–7

Your wisdom is a gift, Father. I ask that You open my mind and heart to receive Your direction for living. I confess that I often try to solve my problems without Your help. Help me be sensitive to Your leading in all the tests and trials I face. You have instructed me to come to You and ask for wisdom, and You will give me everything I need without reproach. Thank You for this generous promise. *Amen.*

THANK GOD *for* HIS FORGIVENESS

Therefore, if anyone is in Christ, he is a new creation; old things have passed away; behold, all things have become new. Now all things are of God, who has reconciled us to Himself through Jesus Christ, and has given us the ministry of reconciliation.

2 CORINTHIANS 5:17–18

Lord, You have promised to forgive me for all my sins if I come to You with a repentant heart and ask to be forgiven. You have even said that those sins will not be remembered ever again. This wonderful gift You have given me through Your mercy opens the door to live each day with joy in my heart and the knowledge that my sins have been forgiven. Let my light so shine that each of my children may see the love of God in me. *Amen.*

When Trouble Walks *in* Your Door

Trust in the L<small>ORD</small> with all your heart, and lean not on your own understanding; in all your ways acknowledge Him, and He shall direct your paths.

P<small>ROVERBS</small> 3:5–6

*F*ather, I recognize that troubles come to each of us in all shapes and sizes. Help me trust in You with all my heart. I will run to You when trouble knocks and seek Your wisdom, for You have promised to direct my path. Give me the wisdom to trust You with all that concerns me. For You, O Lord, are forever faithful. *Amen.*

With God, There Is No Room *for* Fear

The Lord is my light and my salvation;
whom shall I fear? The Lord is the strength of
my life; of whom shall I be afraid? . . . Though
an army may encamp against me, my heart
shall not fear; though war may rise against
me, in this I will be confident.

Psalm 27:1, 3

Savior, You have said, "Perfect love casts out fear" (1 John 4:18). I receive this promise and look forward each day to accepting Your saving grace and experiencing what You have planned for me. Please give each one in my family the reassurance that nothing is too difficult for You. Instill in them the confidence to come boldly to the throne of grace to worship You. *Amen.*

GIVE ME COURAGE *and* INTEGRITY

Dishonest scales are an abomination to the
LORD, but a just weight is His delight. When
pride comes, then comes shame; but with
the humble is wisdom. The integrity of the
upright will guide them, but the perversity of
the unfaithful will destroy them.

PROVERBS 11:1–3

I know that honesty and integrity are essential qualities of a father's life. Heavenly Father, place within my heart the desire to serve You faithfully with courage and integrity in every area of my life. I want my children to see You in all that I do. I confess that I cannot do this alone. Therefore, I rest in the power of Your presence, leaning on You to be my Guide as I speak honestly and boldly of Your love, mercy, and grace. *Amen.*

An Everyday Father

Jesus said to him, "'You shall love the Lord
your God with all your heart, with all your
soul, and with all your mind.' This is the first
and great commandment. And the second
is like it: 'You shall love your neighbor as
yourself.' On these two commandments hang
all the Law and the Prophets."

MATTHEW 22:37–40

*D*ear Lord, I need Your guidance every moment of every day to be the father You wish me to be. Through Your Word, You have asked me to love You with all my heart, with all my soul, and with all my mind. Help me be aware of Your presence and let me live in such a way that all of my family will grow to have a love for Your Word and will desire to walk closely with You. *Amen.*

EVERYTHING BEGINS
with TRUST

And he said:
"The Lord is my rock and my fortress and my
deliverer; the God of my strength, in whom
I will trust; my shield and the horn of my
salvation, my stronghold and my refuge; my
Savior, You save me from violence."

2 SAMUEL 22:2–3

*Y*ou have promised to be my strength,
Lord, and asked me to trust in You
with all my heart. I confess I need Your pro-
tection and guidance in my life every day.
Place within my heart the desire to seek
Your face in everything I do. I realize the
triumphs in life come through the workings
of Your Spirit when I put my trust in You.
You are the irresistible force that nothing
can oppose. *Amen.*

GRATITUDE BEGINS
with ATTITUDE

Finally, brethren, whatever things are true,
whatever things are noble, whatever things are
just, whatever things are pure, whatever things
are lovely, whatever things are of good report,
if there is any virtue and if there is anything
praiseworthy—meditate on these things.

PHILIPPIANS 4:8

Almighty God, sometimes I find that my life is overwhelming and my attitude is negative. Please forgive me and fill my life with the power of Your presence. You have asked me to meditate on things that are true, noble, just, and pure. Frankly, I cannot do any of that without Your Spirit leading my life. Help me accept that this transformation begins in the mind and transcends into an attitude of gratitude when I walk with You, for You are my everything. *Amen.*

The Gift *of* Kindness

*"Or what man is there among you who, if
his son asks for bread, will give him a stone?
Or if he asks for a fish, will he give him a
serpent? If you then, being evil, know how to
give good gifts to your children, how much
more will your Father who is in heaven give
good things to those who ask Him!"*

MATTHEW 7:9–11

Lord, give me a spirit of kindness, first with my family and also with others with whom I come in contact each day. I recognize that everyone craves love and encouragement. Help me demonstrate Your love through kindness and a caring heart. Through You I want to build confidence, security, and a foundation of trust for my family that cannot be broken. Let my words and actions reflect Your love, grace, and mercy. *Amen.*

The COMFORT ONLY GOD CAN GIVE

Blessed be the God and Father of our Lord Jesus Christ, the Father of mercies and God of all comfort, who comforts us in all our tribulation, that we may be able to comfort those who are in any trouble, with the comfort with which we ourselves are comforted by God.

2 CORINTHIANS 1:3–4

*Y*ou are the God of all comfort. Sometimes I face so many unexpected circumstances that I ask the question, "Why me, Lord?" Father, I know You have promised never to leave me or forsake me, and You are the One who comforts us in all our tribulations. For this I thank You. Place within my heart the desire to share Your comfort with those around me who are facing trials and tribulations. I will faithfully serve You. *Amen.*

YOU ARE MY STRENGTH

*For I am persuaded that neither death nor
life, nor angels nor principalities nor powers,
nor things present nor things to come, nor
height nor depth, nor any other created thing,
shall be able to separate us from the love of
God which is in Christ Jesus our Lord.*

ROMANS 8:38–39

Lord, as a father, my life is filled with joy, happiness, peace, challenges, trials, sorrow, worry, fear, and doubt. I realize that these are common in every father's life. You have promised that nothing can separate us from Your love, and I thank You for that promise. I will begin each day praising You for Your love and look forward to sharing that love with my family and friends. *Amen.*

My Challenge: *To Grow in My Walk with God*

Teach me, O Lord, the way of Your statutes, and I shall keep it to the end. Give me understanding, and I shall keep Your law; indeed, I shall observe it with my whole heart. Make me walk in the path of Your commandments, for I delight in it.

Psalm 119:33–35

*E*verlasting Father, I confess that sometimes I find it hard to grow in my walk with You. My life is filled with distractions that draw me away from You. Teach me the way of Your statutes and place within my heart a hunger for the understanding of Your Word. Help me walk in the path of Your commandments, for You are my delight and in You all things are possible. *Amen.*

A Father's Character Begins *with* Honesty

Lying lips are an abomination to the Lord, but those who deal truthfully are His delight.

PROVERBS 12:22

You keep Your promises and never lie. Lord, I ask that you give me the same discipline to always be honest and truthful with my family and those with whom I come in contact. Help me guard my words and be the example for my family that will bring honor and glory to Your name. I ask that Your Spirit direct my path for Your glory. I thank You for the blessings You daily give to me. *Amen.*

Forgiveness:
A Gift *of* God's Love

As far as the east is from the west,
so far has He removed our transgressions from us.

Psalm 103:12

You have promised to remove my sins from me as far as the east is from the west, O Lord. For this gift, I thank You. Open my heart to forget what lies behind me and live each day knowing that I have been forgiven of all my shortcomings through the precious blood of Jesus. Help me be as forgiving of others as You have been of me so that nothing will keep me from living in the center of Your will. *Amen.*

A Father's Faith

And let us not grow weary while doing
good, for in due season we shall reap if we
do not lose heart. Therefore, as we have
opportunity, let us do good to all, especially
to those who are of the household of faith.

GALATIANS 6:9–10

God, You have chosen to make me the spiritual leader of my family. My greatest desire is to be faithful to the calling You have given me. Be my guiding light and fill me with the power of Your presence. May I faithfully serve You, fulfill the responsiblities of leading my family, and be the father You wish for me to be. *Amen.*

LORD, HEAR MY PRAYER

"Ask, and it will be given to you; seek, and you will find; knock, and it will be opened to you. For everyone who asks receives, and he who seeks finds, and to him who knocks it will be opened."

MATTHEW 7:7–8

*L*ord, You have asked me to come to You with an open heart, to seek You and find what is Your will for my life. Help me be open and sincere with all that I am for Your glory. Through Your grace and goodness, lead me to a deeper, richer relationship with You. Mold me to be the father You wish me to be. Fill me with Your wisdom and understanding so that Your Word will come alive in my life. Place Your hand upon me so that Your Spirit will be my constant guide and so that You may be glorified in all that I say and do. May You forever be praised. *Amen.*

FATHER, HELP ME
BE PATIENT

*My brethren, count it all joy when you fall
into various trials, knowing that the testing
of your faith produces patience. But let
patience have its perfect work, that you may
be perfect and complete, lacking nothing.*

JAMES 1:2–4

Heavenly Father, I recognize that sometimes my emotions get in the way of being patient with my family, friends, and job. Your Word says, "Wait on the LORD; be of good courage, and He shall strengthen your heart; wait, I say, on the LORD!" (Psalm 27:14). Help me accept these words and patiently wait for You, especially when I am in the middle of a difficult situation that I cannot control, for I know that You will grant me all the patience I will ever need. *Amen.*

Worship *the* Lord

*"But the hour is coming, and now is, when
the true worshipers will worship the Father in
spirit and truth; for the Father is seeking such
to worship Him. God is Spirit, and those who
worship Him must worship in spirit and truth."*

John 4:23–24

*Y*ou are my everything, O Lord, and
every blessing I receive comes directly
from You. I know that my relationship with
You grows out of worship, reading Scripture,
and the power of the Holy Spirit working
within me. Help me come to You with an
open heart and a willingness to surrender my
life to You. Refresh my spirit and draw me
closer to You. Place within my heart a desire
to worship You daily, and as I walk more
closely with You, help me have an impact on
my loved ones for Your glory. *Amen.*

PERFECT LOVE CASTS *Out* FEAR

Be strong and of good courage, do not fear
nor be afraid of them; for the LORD your
God, He is the One who goes with you. He
will not leave you nor forsake you.

DEUTERONOMY 31:6

*F*ather, You clearly say in Your Word
that "there is no fear in love; but perfect love casts out fear" (1 John 4:18). Thank
You for the gift of Your love, which is not
merely a warm sentiment or feeling; it is a
living, active force that changes who we are.
I know that You are with me both in the
easiest of times and the most difficult times.
Even when I feel uncertain about the future,
let me never be afraid, for Your love is greater
than anything I will ever face. *Amen.*

YOUR PROTECTION:
A FATHER'S GIFT

My soul, wait silently for God alone, for my
expectation is from Him. He only is my rock and
my salvation; He is my defense; I shall not be
moved. In God is my salvation and my glory; the
rock of my strength, and my refuge, is in God.

PSALM 62:5–7

*Y*ou are my rock and my salvation.
Lord, I know I can come to You each
day and You will listen to my requests, my
problems, my needs, and everything that
goes on in my life. You have promised to be
available to me always when I trust in You
with all my heart. Let nothing separate me
from Your love. Help me show Your loving
grace and mercy to everyone in my family
each day as I live according to Your Word.
You are my everything. *Amen.*

My Jesus

"I am the vine, you are the branches. He who abides in Me, and I in him, bears much fruit; for without Me you can do nothing. If anyone does not abide in Me, he is cast out as a branch and is withered; and they gather them and throw them into the fire, and they are burned. If you abide in Me, and My words abide in you, you will ask what you desire, and it shall be done for you."

JOHN 15:5–7

Just as you say in Your Word, Father, You are the vine, and we are the branches. I accept that I am forever connected to You and nothing can separate me from Your love. Open my eyes that I might see how I can best serve You. Help me abide in Your Word that I might grow in grace with You and bear fruit for Your glory. I thank You for Your love and patience with me. Let each day be filled with Your presence as we walk together to fulfill Your purpose. *Amen.*

GOD'S PROMISE *to* YOU

*Behold, this day I am going the way of all the
earth. And you know in all your hearts and in
all your souls that not one thing has failed of
all the good things which the LORD your God
spoke concerning you. All have come to pass
for you; not one word of them has failed.*

JOSHUA 23:14

As I search the Scripture, O Lord, I
see that You have given me many
promises to guide my steps and help me live
each moment for You. To know that You will
never leave me nor forsake me is such a blessing. You have also said, "Delight yourself also
in the LORD, and He shall give you the desires
of your heart" (Psalm 37:4). I praise Your
holy name, and accept that each one of Your
promises has been uttered to help me grow in
my faith and draw me closer to You. *Amen.*

A FATHER'S LIFE

For the Scripture says, "Whoever believes on Him will not be put to shame." For there is no distinction between Jew and Greek, for the same Lord over all is rich to all who call upon Him.

ROMANS 10:11–12

I have been given the privilege of becoming a father. This is a gift that only You can give, Lord. Through Your divine providence, I now have children to teach, nurture, and raise. Guide me so that I might place the love of God in their hearts. I want very much to be the best father I can be, and I recognize that I need the guidance of Your Spirit to fulfill the task You have given me. You have promised that everything I need to be a responsible father is available through Your Word. Open my eyes and heart to receive Your direction. *Amen.*

A FATHER'S FAITH IS *the* KEY

*But without faith it is impossible to
please Him, for he who comes to God
must believe that He is, and that He is a
rewarder of those who diligently seek Him.*

HEBREWS 11:6

Heavenly Father, I confess that I need Your direction and power in my life. I am not capable of handling all of my responsibilities alone. I trust in You and depend on Your Spirit to guide my steps to fulfill all of my duties. I know that everything You have promised in Your Word is true. No matter what life brings my way, I can come to You, and You will always be there for me. Thank You for Your love, mercy, and grace. *Amen.*

The Choice Is Yours

*"No one can serve two masters; for either he
will hate the one and love the other, or else he
will be loyal to the one and despise the other.
You cannot serve God and mammon."*

MATTHEW 6:24

So many times in life I struggle with my priorities, my needs, and my wants. Father, I often find myself placing personal desires before my spiritual responsibilities. You have said we cannot serve two masters. Help me look to You first and foremost in every area of my life. Place within my heart the desire to serve You and to lead my family in such a way that You will always be lifted up. I recognize that the choice is mine; help me always choose You. *Amen.*

An EXTRAORDINARY FATHER

*For we are His workmanship, created in Christ
Jesus for good works, which God prepared
beforehand that we should walk in them.*

EPHESIANS 2:10

I want to be the best father I can be,
O Lord. I was created in Your image
with the mission to do good works. You
know me from the inside out, and there is
nothing hidden from You. I am Your mas-
terpiece. Please paint the portrait of my life
in such a way that I will bring honor and
glory to You. I know that through You, all
things are possible. Lead me in every area
of my life to be a part of Your perfect plan.
Amen.

LIVING *for* GOD *from the* INSIDE *Out*

Therefore we do not lose heart. Even though our outward man is perishing, yet the inward man is being renewed day by day.

2 CORINTHIANS 4:16

Lord, You have asked me to live each day for You. I recognize that I can only do this if You change my heart and help me be a different person. Guide me to walk, talk, and interact with my family and friends in such a way that You will be reflected in my life. You have called me to live for You and have promised that what I do matters in Your kingdom. As Your bond-servant, pleasing You is my greatest desire. I acknowledge that as a Christian father, who I am in Christ will be reflected in my children in the way I live from the inside out. *Amen.*

HONOR BEGINS *with* GOD

*Honor the LORD with your possessions, and with
the firstfruits of all your increase; so your barns
will be filled with plenty, and your vats will
overflow with new wine.*

PROVERBS 3:9–10

Lord, I realize that every possession I have belongs to You. Open my heart and mind to be sensitive to those around me who are less fortunate than I am. You have asked us through Your Word to honor You with all we have, and You will provide a way to bless others who are struggling in life. Give me a spirit of servanthood that I might reach out and help someone else to know You and experience the unconditional love only You can give. *Amen.*

GOD IS WATCHING

Where can I go from Your Spirit? Or where can I flee from Your presence? If I ascend into heaven, You are there; if I make my bed in hell, behold, You are there. If I take the wings of the morning, and dwell in the uttermost parts of the sea, even there Your hand shall lead me, and Your right hand shall hold me.

PSALM 139:7–10

*F*ather God, I know that nothing in life is hidden from You. Whatever challenges I encounter, You will be there to carry me through. Even when I face situations I do not understand or comprehend, You will be there. Give me the direction I need to glorify You and live in the power of Your presence. I confess that I am helpless without You, and only through Your strength and power can I glorify Your holy name. *Amen.*

A Father's Reward

But the fruit of the Spirit is love, joy,
peace, longsuffering, kindness, goodness,
faithfulness, gentleness, self-control.
Against such there is no law.

Galatians 5:22–23

*L*ord, You are calling me as a Christian father to walk in the Spirit of love with those in my family. Help me live a transparent life so that I might show the fruit of Your Spirit. I gratefully accept that if I live a God-centered life and make Christ a priority, You will give me the fruit of Your Spirit. I know that only You can change my heart and give me the peace that passes all understanding. I surrender all to You and ask You to fill me with Your Spirit. *Amen.*

A FATHER'S LEGACY

The righteous man walks in his integrity;
His children are blessed after him.

PROVERBS 20:7

As a father, I desire to be a man of integrity, that I might be a reflection of Your mercy and grace, O Lord. You have called me to do what is right and to live according to Your Word. Guide my steps each day to walk in wisdom and bring honor and glory to Your holy name. The legacy I leave will be determined by the life I lead and the love I demonstrate for the One who gave His life so that I might have eternal life. Help me be faithful to the calling You have given me. *Amen.*

A Father's Prayer
Changes Everything

Confess your trespasses to one another,
and pray for one another, that you may be
healed. The effective, fervent prayer of a
righteous man avails much.

James 5:16

ather, someone has said that prayer is like the breath of life, and I cannot exist spiritually without it. You have asked me to connect with other Christians to confess my trespasses and pray with and for each other. Help me be open with my family and those I care about and love. Remind me that through prayer, You give me direction. When I am open to sharing anything and everything with You, changes will be evident, and You will be glorified. *Amen.*

The GREAT PHYSICIAN

*So Jesus answered and said to them,
"Assuredly, I say to you, if you have faith and
do not doubt, you will not only do what was
done to the fig tree, but also if you say to this
mountain, 'Be removed and be cast into the
sea,' it will be done. And whatever things you
ask in prayer, believing, you will receive."*

MATTHEW 21:21–22

There is a saying that when you "fight all your battles on your knees, you will win every time." Father, I come to You to find healing for my spirit and my physical body. I know You want the best for me as I walk closely with You, trusting You in every situation. James 4:7–8 says, "Submit to God. Resist the devil and he will flee from you." You have asked me to take the first step. Lord, I am running to You with open arms. Heal my mind, body, and spirit that I may be all that You have called me to be. *Amen.*

LIVE *for* TODAY

"Do not remember the former things, nor consider the things of old. Behold, I will do a new thing, now it shall spring forth; shall you not know it? I will even make a road in the wilderness and rivers in the desert."

ISAIAH 43:18–19

My Savior, I confess that I have not always lived for You, and there are memories I would like to forget. Help me put the past behind me and live for today and every day in Your presence. You have said, "If anyone is in Christ, he is a new creation; old things have passed away; behold, all things have become new" (2 Corinthians 5:17). Thank You for forgetting my past and all the mistakes I have made. Fill me with the power of Your Spirit that I might walk in Your presence and serve Your purpose. *Amen.*

LORD, GUARD MY TONGUE

Death and life are in the power of the tongue,
and those who love it will eat its fruit.

PROVERBS 18:21

*F*ather, help me choose carefully the words I speak to my wife, my children, and those I love. I recognize that words can either build up or tear down their confidence. I know that the words I speak to my family will leave a lasting impression and have a great impact on who my children will become. Let me encourage them every day and share with them the love of Christ. It is always in Your precious holy Name that I ask these things, Lord. *Amen.*

BUILDING BLOCKS *for* YOUR CHILDREN

The heart of the wise teaches his mouth,
and adds learning to his lips. Pleasant
words are like a honeycomb, sweetness to
the soul and health to the bones.

PROVERBS 16:23–24

O Lord, I know that hugs and words of encouragement are the building blocks my children need. I recognize that their self-image and confidence depends on how I interact with them. Help me create a habit of letting them know how special they are in Your eyes and how proud I am of them. Place within my heart the tender, loving words You wish for them to hear as I seek Your wisdom and direction. *Amen.*

Unconditional Love

*So husbands ought to love their own
wives as their own bodies; he who loves
his wife loves himself.*

EPHESIANS 5:28

*And you, fathers, do not provoke your
children to wrath, but bring them up in
the training and admonition of the Lord.*

EPHESIANS 6:4

*W*onderful Counselor, You have assured me that You love me just the way I am. Help me demonstrate that same love to my wife and children. I realize that I must love my wife with the same love I have for myself. Give me the insight to be sensitive to her needs with patience and understanding. My children are my pride and joy, therefore let me surround them in an atmosphere of unconditional love. *Amen.*